The Will
Of God
In Prayer

Kenneth E. Hagin

Unless otherwise indicated, all Scripture quotations in this volume are from the *King James Version* of the Bible.

Third Printing 2002

ISBN 0-89276-066-4

In the U.S. write:
Kenneth Hagin Ministries
P.O. Box 50126
Tulsa, OK 74150-0126
1-888-28-FAITH
www.rhema.org

In Canada write:
Kenneth Hagin Ministries
P.O. Box 335, Station D,
Etobicoke (Toronto), Ontario
Canada, M9A 4X3

Contents

The Six Most Important Things in Prayer (Part 1)

Bible Texts: John 16:23,24; Mark 11:24-26; Acts 27:25

Central Truth: "There is something about believing God that will cause Him to pass over a million people to get to you."
— Smith Wigglesworth

Many times I have asked people, as they got up from praying, what they believed. Often they have answered "Well, I *hope* God heard me." I tell them He didn't.

In His Word He says, "If you *believe* you shall receive," not "If you *hope* you shall receive." He didn't say to "keep on keeping on" until you got the answer. He said when you pray you should believe you receive.

When you believe you receive, you don't have to pray all night long. You can go to bed and sleep peacefully, knowing God has heard you and will answer your prayer. It's the most wonderful thing in the world to be able to pillow your head on the promises of God and sleep like a baby. Everything around you might be in turmoil, but in the midst of it you can have peace.

This lesson deals with the six most important things the Christian should know about prayer.

Number 1: Pray to the Father in the Name of Jesus

JOHN 16:23,24
23 And in that day ye shall ask me nothing. Verily, verily, I say unto you, Whatsoever ye shall ask the Father in my name, he will give it you.
24 Hitherto have ye asked nothing in my name: ask, and ye shall receive, that your joy may be full.

When Jesus spoke these words, He was here on earth. He was talking about the day in which we live.

He had not yet gone to Calvary. He had not died and been buried. He had not risen from the dead. The

New Covenant was not in force. His blood had not been carried into the Holy of Holies. (His blood is the seal of the Covenant.)

Man had the promise of redemption, but had not received it. Eternal life had been promised, but had not been provided. None had the New Birth — they only had the promise of it, because the New Birth is available only under the New Covenant.

This New Covenant was prophesied about in the Old Covenant. Under the Old Covenant, men's hearts never were changed. That's the reason they kept on sinning. They couldn't help but sin.

Some of the greatest saints of the Old Testament sinned. After they were forgiven for one sin, they would commit another. Their natures were all wrong; their hearts were all wrong. They only had a covering for their sins.

But God promised in His Word that He would take that old heart out of us and give us a new one. He said He would put a new spirit in us (Ezek. 11:19). This became available under the New Covenant.

In John 16:23,24, Jesus told His disciples that after He went to Calvary and was raised from the dead, people were to pray to His Father.

Prayer based on legal grounds should be addressed to the Father in the Name of Jesus. We are not supposed to pray to Jesus. This was His instruction.

The disciples asked Him, while He was here on earth, to teach them to pray. He taught them to say, "Our Father. . . ." We refer to this as the Lord's Prayer (Matt. 6:9-13), but it is not New Testament prayer.

This prayer didn't ask a thing in Jesus' Name; His Name wasn't even mentioned. *This prayer was prayed under the Old Covenant.* Under the New Covenant, which was sealed with the precious blood of Jesus, we are to pray to the Father in Jesus' Name.

Now let us focus our attention on the word "whatsoever" in John 16:23. Often we say we are believing for an answer to prayer "if it is God's will." But this verse makes no such condition. On the contrary, it says, *"Whatsoever ye shall ask the Father in my name, he will give it you."* It must have been His will; otherwise, He wouldn't have said it!

Why did Jesus say, *"Whatsoever ye shall ask the Father in my name, he will give it you"*? The answer is found in verse 24: *". . . that your joy may be full."*

Our joy certainly can't be full if we are out of work and our children are hungry. Our joy can't be full if our bodies are racked with pain. Our joy can't be full if there are problems in our home.

Jesus said the Father would give us *"whatsoever"* we ask so our *"joy may be full."*

But there is a seat to success with this kind of praying. The key is in the words, *"Whatsoever ye shall ASK THE FATHER IN MY NAME. . . ."* We are to address our prayers to the Father in the Name of Jesus.

Number 2: Believe You Receive

MARK 11:24
24 Therefore I say unto you, What things soever ye desire, when ye pray, believe that ye receive them, and ye shall have them.

Smith Wigglesworth once said there is something about believing God that will cause Him to pass over a million people to get to you.

God is a faith God. We are faith children of a faith God. He works on the principle of faith.

We are saved by faith: *"For by grace are ye saved through faith; and that not of yourselves: it is the gift of God: Not of works, lest any man should boast"* (Eph. 2:8,9).

We walk by faith, not by sight. It is the prayer of faith God listens to. He said you can have the desires of your heart if you believe you receive them. You have to believe first, however.

Most people want to receive and then they will believe. But it is the other way around: *The believing part comes first.*

I am convinced that if people would quit praying repeatedly about some of the things they pray about and begin thanking God for the answer, the answer would come right away. But they keep on praying in unbelief.

If a person asks for the same thing again, he doesn't believe he received it the first time he asked. If he believed he had received it, he would be thanking God for it, and it would be made manifest.

The faith Jesus was talking about in Mark 11 is heart faith — a spiritual faith — not head faith. We get used to walking by head faith. But we are to believe in our heart that we receive what we are praying for, even though we do not see the answer with our physical eyes.

This also is true of physical healing, but it seems more difficult to practice faith for physical healing than for anything else, because we have the body, with all its feelings and symptoms, to contend with.

Most people will believe God has healed them when they can see their condition has grown better, or when the symptoms are gone. Anyone can believe what he can see. What Jesus was teaching here is that we should believe when we pray and *then* we will receive.

For many years I have practiced this kind of faith, and Mark 11:24 has been my standby. I have experienced it in my own life as I have prayed for the desires of my heart, believing that I receive them. It is true not only for healing, but also in every other area of life. No matter what the need may be — material, spiritual, or financial — this is the way we receive.

Smith Wigglesworth said some people are ready to give up if their prayers aren't answered immediately. But, he said, this proves that they never believed God in the first place.

Often God permits our faith to be tried and tested right up to the end. When you believe God, you can stand firm, even though you are tested.

I have been there and I know by experience. I learned many years ago to laugh all the more when the going gets rough. I don't always *feel* like laughing, but I make myself laugh right in the face of the devil. I smile and say that I believe God.

When Paul was on a ship bound for Rome, a great storm arose. Because the ship was in danger of sinking, the crew attempted to lighten it by throwing cargo

overboard. This didn't help the situation, and the storm continued, night and day, for "many days." Finally the crew and passengers gave up all hope that they or the ship would survive. However, right in the midst of the storm's fury, Paul addressed them, saying he believed God:

ACTS 27:26
25 Wherefore, sirs, be of good cheer. for I believe God, that it be even as it was told me.

You and I may not have to face a storm-tossed sea, but we do have to face storms in life. We, too, can stand with the faith of Paul and announce that we believe God.

Number 3:
Forgive When You Pray

MARK 11:25,26
25 And when ye stand praying, forgive, if ye have ought against any: that your Father also which is in heaven may forgive you your trespasses.
26 But if ye do not forgive, neither will your Father which is in heaven forgive your trespasses.

Before we can expect an answer to our prayers, we must forgive any who may have wronged us. We cannot hold a grudge — we cannot keep an unforgiving spirit — if we want our prayers to reach God's throne of grace.

Prayer will not work in an unforgiving heart. No one can have an effective prayer life and have anything in his heart against another. You cannot have hatred in your heart. You cannot have revenge in your heart.

You are not responsible for that other person's life. You are responsible only for *your* life. What is in another person's heart can't hinder you, but what you have in your heart against him can hinder you.

We must watch our inward man with all diligence. We cannot afford to allow a root of bitterness, a bit of envy, or a spark of revenge to get in there. It will wreck our spiritual life. It will stall our prayer life. It will mar our faith and eventually it will shipwreck us.

A fellow once wanted me to pray that he never would have any more trouble with the devil. I told him I didn't know anyone who was free from trouble with the devil, least of all me.

We can't pray that we won't have any more trouble with the devil, but we can learn to take authority over him: *"Resist the devil and he will flee from you"* (James 4:7).

God prepares a table before us in the presence of our enemies. Jesus is there right in the presence of the devil. Right in the presence of the enemies of doubt and despair, we can sit at the table of victory and deliverance with Jesus. In the face of adverse circumstances we can believe we receive.

Memory Text:
"Praying always with all prayer and supplication in the Spirit, and watching thereunto with all perseverance and supplication for all saints."
— Eph. 6:18

The Six Most Important Things in Prayer (Part 2)

Bible Texts: Romans 8:26,27; 1 Corinthians 14:14,15; Jude 20; 1 Corinthians 14:4

Central Truth: When we allow the Holy Spirit to pray through us — to help us in our prayer life — we will see amazing answers to our prayers.

Praying always with all prayer and supplication in the Spirit and watching thereunto with all perseverance and supplication for all saints.
— Ephesians 6:18

Dr. James Moffatt's translation of Ephesians 6:18, quoted above, says, "praying at all times . . . with all manner of prayer. . . ." Another modern translation says, "praying with all kinds of prayer."

The *King James Version*, even though it does not say "all kinds of prayer," says *"praying always with all prayer,"* inferring that there is more than one kind of prayer. If there were not, it merely would have said, "praying always," and would have stopped there.

How desperately our nation needs prayer. How desperately the church needs prayer. How desperately we individuals need prayer. Nothing can take the place of prayer for meeting the needs of our family.

In our last lesson we discussed three points in our study of the six most important things the Christian should know about prayer. They were: (1) pray to the Father in the Name of Jesus; (2) believe you receive; and (3) forgive when you pray. This lesson will cover the last three points in this topic.

Number 4: Depend Upon the Holy Spirit in Your Prayer Life

ROMANS 8:26,27
26 Likewise the Spirit also helpeth our infirmities: for we know not what we should pray for as we

ought: but the Spirit itself maketh intercession for us with groanings which cannot be uttered.

27 And he that searcheth the hearts knoweth what is the mind of the Spirit, because he maketh intercession for the saints according to the will of God.

1 CORINTHIANS 14:14,15

14 For if I pray in an unknown tongue, my spirit prayeth, but my understanding is unfruitful.

15 What is it then? I will pray with the spirit, and I will pray with the understanding also: I will sing with the spirit, and I will sing with the understanding also.

Christians everywhere pray with the understanding, but not all pray with the Spirit (pray in tongues). Many do not know it is even possible to do so.

Some in their haste and their ignorance of the Scriptures have said that tongues have been done away with. But if that were true, how are we to "pray with the spirit" today? Surely the Corinthian Christians didn't have a means of praying that we can't have. We have the same means available to us today.

Paul said that when he prayed in an unknown tongue, his spirit prayed. *When you pray in tongues, it is your spirit praying by the Holy Spirit within you.* Likewise, your

groaning is the Holy Spirit within you groaning. I sometimes have been so burdened in prayer that I didn't have adequate words to express my feelings. All I could do was groan from somewhere way down deep inside me. Paul says these groanings that escape our lips come from our spirit — our innermost being. When this happens, it is the Spirit helping us pray, as we see in Romans 8:26.

According to the late P. C. Nelson, the literal Greek translation of Romans 8:26 says, "The Spirit Himself maketh intercession for us with groanings that cannot be uttered in articulate speech." Articulate speech means your regular kind of speech. Speaking with tongues is *not* your regular kind of speech, so this verse includes speaking and praying with other tongues.

Paul said the Holy Spirit would help us in our prayer life. Why? ". . . for we know not what we should pray for as we ought: but the Spirit itself maketh intercession for us. . . ." (Rom. 8:26).

We do not always understand everything concerning what we are praying about, but the Holy Spirit does. When we allow Him to pray through us — to help us in our prayer life — we will see amazing answers to our prayers!

If I know specific details about what I'm praying for, I can believe when I pray, and I will receive them. However, sometimes there are things we know we need to pray about, but we do not know how to pray for them. The Holy Spirit knows, and He can help us. (It is easier to have faith for needs like rent and groceries because we know what we are praying for. But there are other situations in life that aren't so easy to pray for.)

There have been times in my own life when I have told the Lord I didn't know exactly how I should pray concerning my children. When I know there is a problem, I begin praying in tongues, and most of the time before I get through, I have the answer.

Number 5: Pray the Prayer of Intercession

This point ties in closely with Number 4. Romans 8:26 says, ". . . *the Spirit itself maketh intercession for us with groanings which cannot be uttered.*" The prayer of intercession is not for you. *An intercessor is one who takes the place of another.* You are interceding for another.

Every Spirit-filled believer can expect the Holy Spirit to help him intercede. This intercession can be for someone's salvation, healing, etc. It even includes praying for things or people we don't know about, but the Holy Spirit does.*

After a time of praying in the Spirit we will know whether we were praying in tongues for ourselves — to build ourselves up spiritually and worship God, which is discussed in the next step — or we were interceding for others.

On occasion — and sometimes over a period of time — I have had a burden of intercession before I even knew for whom I was praying. I can tell when I am in intercession or travail for someone who is lost.

(When you take the place of a lost person in intercession, you will experience that same lost feeling in your own spirit. As you pray in the Spirit, interceding for the person, the Holy Spirit will deal with his heart and bring him under conviction of sin.)

Number 6: Edify Yourself by Praying in the Holy Spirit

JUDE 20
20 But ye, beloved, building up yourselves on your most holy faith praying in the Holy Ghost.

1 CORINTHIANS 14:4
4 He that speaketh in an unknown tongue edifieth himself. . . .

There is one phase of speaking with tongues in our prayer life that is neither praying for someone else nor interceding for anyone else. It is purely a means of personal spiritual edification. It aids us spiritually and edifies us. We all need this kind of praying. We cannot help others — we cannot edify others — unless we ourselves have been edified.

Praying in this manner has a three-fold value. First, it is a means of spiritual edification. It affects us individually. Second, it is a means of praying for things about which we do not know. Third, the Holy Spirit helps us make intercession.

Speaking in tongues is not only an initial evidence of the Holy Spirit's indwelling; it is a continual experience for the rest of one's life. It is to assist in the worship of God. It is a flowing stream that never should dry up. It will enrich your life spiritually.

✳

Memory Text:

"Praying always with all prayer and supplication in the Spirit and watching thereunto with all perseverance and supplication for all saints."
— Eph. 6:18

---

*For a complete study of this subject, see Rev. Kenneth E. Hagin's book *The Art of Intercession.*

What Jesus Said About Prayer (Part 1)

Bible Text: Matthew 6:5-13

Central Truth: The Lord's Prayer is a pattern in which we see certain principles of prayer.

While Jesus was here on earth, He taught much about prayer. Perhaps the best known of His teachings on prayer is the often-repeated "Lord's Prayer." In this brief prayer, we find a pattern for prayer which Jesus gave to His disciples.

Just preceding this prayer, as recorded in Matthew's Gospel, are a few verses which also are very enlightening on this subject. They actually are a prelude to the prayer.

MATTHEW 6:5-13

5 And when thou prayest, thou shalt not be as the hypocrites are: for they love to pray standing in the synagogues and in the corners of the streets, that they may be seen of men. Verily I say unto you, They have their reward.

6 But thou, when thou prayest, enter into thy closet, and when thou hast shut thy door, pray to thy Father which is in secret; and thy Father which seeth in secret shall reward thee openly.

7 But when ye pray, use not vain repetitions, as the heathen do: for they think that they shall be heard for their much speaking.

8 Be not ye therefore like unto them: for your Father knoweth what things ye have need of, before ye ask him.

9 After this manner therefore pray ye: Our Father which art in heaven, Hallowed be thy name.

10 Thy kingdom come. Thy will be done in earth, as it is in heaven.

11 Give us this day our daily bread.

12 And forgive us our debts, as we forgive our debtors.

13 And lead us not into temptation, but deliver us from evil: For thine is

the kingdom, and the power, and the glory, for ever. Amen.

Private Prayer

One of the first things Jesus said here was, *"And when thou prayest, thou shalt not be as the hypocrites are. . . ."* Surely none of us wants to be hypocritical, especially in our praying. Then He described the hypocrite: *". . . they love to pray standing in the synagogues and in the corners of the streets, that they may be seen of men."*

This does not mean, however, that all of our praying should be private. We can look at the Early Church in prayer and see them praying together as a group throughout the Book of Acts.

What Jesus was referring to here was the danger of praying only to be seen of men. There are those who pray in public to appear really spiritual; to make people think they are real prayer warriors. Those who pray only for the applause of men have their reward, and that is all it is — the fleeting applause of men.

Jesus told His disciples to *"enter into thy closet and when thou hast shut thy door, pray to thy Father which is in secret."* He was stressing the importance of a private prayer life.

Public prayer is necessary and vital in the life of the Church.

Praying together as a family is necessary and vital to the spiritual strength of the home. But private prayer is essential to the spiritual life of the individual. It is when we grow in spiritual stature. It should not be just at those crisis times when we are driven to our knees. We should be spiritually prepared for such times through a daily prayer time which we set aside for fellowship with God.

Repetitious Prayer

Jesus went on to say, *"But when ye pray, use not vain repetitions, as the heathen do: for they think that they shall be heard for their much speaking"* (v. 7).

Thus, we have two admonitions from the Lord: (1) don't be like the hypocrites in our praying, and (2) don't be like the heathen in our praying.

Jesus said the heathen think they will be heard by their gods because of their repetitious praying. Sad to say, some of this heathen thinking has sifted down into Christian thinking! Many have the idea that God will hear them because of their much speaking — their lengthy and repeated calling on God. They repeat the same prayer — they say the same phrases and words — over and over again, thinking they will be heard because of that. But this is exactly what Jesus condemned when He said, ". . . *use not vain repetitions as the heathen do. . . .*"

Then He said, *"Be not ye therefore like unto them: for your Father knoweth what things ye have need of, before ye ask him."* He knows before you ask, yet He wants you to ask, as we shall see in the next chapter of Matthew, where He said, *"Ask, and it shall be given you. . ."* (Matt. 7:7).

God does not hear you simply because you repeat the same prayer over and over. Some seem to have the idea that if they could just pray long and loudly enough, eventually they could talk God into hearing them. But God is not going to hear you because you prayed loudly or quietly. As we have seen in previous lessons, it is the prayer of faith that God hears. He hears you because you believe Him when you pray, and you come according to His Word.

Basic Principles of Prayer

In the next few verses in Matthew, Jesus taught His disciples some basic elements of prayer. Commonly referred to as the Lord's Prayer, it is more accurately the Disciples' Prayer, or the model for prayer that He gave to them while He walked with them on the earth.

Dispensationally speaking, this is not the Church praying, for the disciples did not ask anything in the Name of Jesus. When the Church prays, she prays in the Name of Jesus. (However, we can learn many truths concerning prayer here.)

Jesus was not telling the disciples to pray this prayer word for word. He was giving them some principles in connection with prayer that will work for the Church today.

The Principle of Praise

The prayer begins with the words, *"Our Father which art in heaven. . . ."* The unsaved can pray this prayer just as they can recite a poem or sing a song. But to really pray this prayer from the heart — to really have fellowship with God — one must actually be a child of God. Otherwise, he cannot truly say, "Our Father. . . ."

We hear much teaching these days about "the fatherhood of God and the brotherhood of man." Some would try to make us believe we all are children of God; that He is the Father of all of us. While it's true that He's the Creator of all, and we all are fellow creatures, He *isn't* the Father of all of us. He is only the Father of those who have been *born again*; those in His family.

During Jesus' earthly ministry He once said to a group of Pharisees, who were very religious people, *"Ye are of your father the devil"* (John 8:44). The Pharisees were good people as far as works were concerned. Yet Jesus said, *"Ye are of your father the devil!"*

Jesus is saying here that the right approach to God is to come to Him because He is our Father, and to come in praise and in worship: *"Our Father which art in heaven, Hallowed be thy name . . ."* (v. 9). Come into His Presence first with praise and worship because He is our Father.

The Principle of Putting God First

The next verse in this pattern prayer says, *"Thy kingdom come. Thy will be done in earth, as it is in heaven"* (v.10). The principle involved here is putting the Kingdom of God first.

Later on in this same chapter, Jesus repeated this principle: *"But seek ye first the kingdom of God, and his righteousness, and all these things shall be added unto you"* (v. 33). If we put God first, we need have no worry about material needs, for *"all these things shall be added unto you."*

We do not have to go through life with the soles of our shoes worn thin, with unpaid bills past due, and driving an old Model T Ford. If God is first in our lives, "all these things shall be added."

Have you ever thought how all-inclusive this prayer is? Jesus prayed, *"Thy kingdom come. THY WILL BE DONE IN EARTH, AS IT IS IN HEAVEN."* Do you suppose there are any sick people in heaven? No. Nor is it God's will that there should be any sick people on earth.

God wants to shower our lives with blessings. He wants our lives here on earth to be lived in the center of His will, as it is in heaven. He wants us to enjoy abundant living. Jesus said, *"I am come that they might have life, and that they might have it more abundantly"* (John 10:10).

The Principle of Daily Prayer

In the next verse of this prayer, Jesus taught us the importance of daily prayer, of asking God for our every need: *"Give us this day our DAILY bread"* (Matt. 6:11). Even though God knows our every need, He still wants us to ask Him!

The Principle of Forgiveness

Jesus taught much about forgiveness during His stay here on earth, and He included forgiveness as one of the essential elements of prayer. *"And forgive us our debts, as we forgive our debtors"* (v. 12). In verses 14 and 15 He also said, *"For if ye forgive men their trespasses, your heavenly Father will also forgive you: But if ye forgive not men their trespasses, neither will your Father forgive your trespasses.*"

Prayer will not work in an unforgiving heart. We simply cannot hold a grudge against anyone and maintain a prayer life that gets results!

There are many instances where mental confusion and emotional frustration can be attributed to harboring bitterness against others. Doctors have learned that people who hold resentment in their hearts are more susceptible to certain types of diseases. When they can get such patients to rid themselves of their resentment, although they have not responded at all to medical treatment, in most cases their trouble clears up. More and more, medical science is discovering how closely our inner feelings are related to our physical health.

I have heard Christians who were not walking in close fellowship with the Lord tell me how badly they had been treated by a certain person. They would say, "Oh, yes, I have *forgiven* him all right, but I never will *forget* what he did to me!" They really hadn't forgiven that person at all! Resentment still lurked in the hidden corners of their heart.

The Principle of Deliverance from Temptation

"*And lead us not into temptation, but deliver us from evil . . .*" (v. 13). The word temptation means "test" or "trial." Many tests and trials could be overcome in advance by the child of God who is enjoying the fellowship with the Father that a proper prayer life brings.

Then we come to the conclusion: "*. . . For thine is the kingdom, and the power, and the glory, for ever. Amen*" (v. 13). The prayer that began with praise also ends with praise.

Memory Text:
"*But seek ye first the kingdom of God, and his righteousness; and all these things shall be added unto you.*"
— Matt. 6:33

What Jesus Said About Prayer (Part 2)

Bible Texts: Matthew 7:7-11; Luke 11:5-13

Central Truth: God loves us and wants us to have good things, just as we love our children and want them to have good things.

The model prayer Jesus gave to His disciples, commonly referred to as the Lord's Prayer (Matt. 6:9-13), begins with the words, *"Our Father which art in heaven. . . ."*

In the next chapter of Matthew, when Jesus was again teaching on prayer, He used another illustration of how the earthly relationship between father and son is like the believer's relationship with the heavenly Father.

MATTHEW 7:7-11

7 Ask, and it shall be given you; seek, and ye shall find; knock, and it shall be opened unto you:
8 For every one that asketh receiveth; and he that seeketh findeth; and to him that knocketh it shall be opened.
9 Or what man is there of you, whom if his son ask bread, will he give him a stone?
10 Or if he ask a fish, will he give him a serpent?
11 If ye then, being evil, know how to give good gifts unto your children, how much more shall your Father which is in heaven give good things to them that ask him?

Knowing God As Father

Here we can see one reason the Jews could not understand Jesus. If Jesus had come along as the prophets of old, proclaiming judgment against them and presenting a distant, unapproachable God to them, they might have understood Him better. That was the picture of God they were accustomed to.

When God came down and talked to Moses on the mountain, there was fire, thunder, and lightning. Anyone who touched that mountain died instantly. When the presence of God moved into the Holy of Holies, no one dared intrude there for fear of instant death. The Jews knew about a God who was high and holy — a God who dealt an awful judgment — and they feared Him.

Jesus, however, came with a message of love. He introduced God as a Father. He suggested they could approach God as a Father. But the Jews just couldn't comprehend that kind of a God.

We see the same thing today. To many, Christianity is just a religion about a faraway God. They really don't know Him. They never have come to Him through Jesus Christ in order to know Him personally as their Father; so they try to approach Him in the wrong manner.

But thank God, He *is* our Father and we can come to Him because we are His children!

Ask, Seek, Knock . . . Believe

Whether or not they use it, most Christians are aware that this verse is in the Bible: *"Ask, and it shall be given you; seek, and ye shall find, knock, and it shall be opened unto you"* (Matt. 7:7).

Too often, though, we fail to receive what we are asking for; we fail to find what we are seeking; and the door on which we are knocking is not opened. Why? We must be doing something wrong when we don't receive, because the next verse promises, *"For every one that asketh receiveth, and he that seeketh findeth; and to him that knocketh it shall be opened"* (v. 8). What is the reason for our failure?

I once read a book by a missionary who had spent 32 years in the Holy Land. This was around the turn of the century, when customs there were very much like they had been for centuries.

In his book, the missionary commented on this passage of Scripture in Matthew 7. He said, "I thought, as most Christians do, that when Jesus said, *'Ask, and it shall be given you; seek, and ye shall find; knock, and it shall be opened unto you,'* He meant if you asked and didn't receive an immediate answer to keep on asking. However, after living in the Holy Land for many years and becoming familiar with the thinking of the Eastern mind, I learned that this was not what Jesus meant at all.

"In those days, if someone came to the outer gate and knocked, seeking entrance, the more wealthy would send their servant to call out and ask the name of the visitor. If it was someone who was known, they could enter immediately. If it was someone unknown, the servant would go to the master of the house and ask if he should let the visitor in. The thought here is that *when you knock, if you are known, you gain immediate entrance. 'To him that knocketh it shall be opened.'* "

If when we ask we do not receive, if when we seek we do not find, if when we knock it is not opened to us, we should ask ourselves if we are known by the Master of the house. If not, we should become acquainted personally and intimately with our Lord and Savior Jesus Christ. We should make Him Lord of our life.

Having done this, the next step is faith, to *". . . believe that he is, and that he is a rewarder of them that diligently seek him"* (Heb. 11:6). For, as Jesus explained in Matthew 7:11, our heavenly Father is eager to give good gifts unto His children: *"If ye then, being evil know how to give good gifts unto your children, how much more shall your Father which is in heaven give good things to them that ask him?"* (v. 11).

What earthly father wants his children to go through life poor and downtrodden, sick and suffering? On the contrary, most of us labor and sacrifice so our children can have advantages we never had. So if you, being carnal — being human — want

good things for your children *". . . HOW MUCH MORE shall your Father which is in heaven give good things to them that ask him?"*

Those three words, "how much more," send a thrill through my spirit. If we want happiness for our children, how much more does God want the same for us. If we want good health for our children, how much more does God want good health for us. If we want material blessings for our children, how much more does God want the same for us.

Luke's account of this story gives us a few more details.

LUKE 11:5-13
5 And he said unto them, Which of you shall have a friend, and shall go unto him at midnight, and say unto him, Friend, lend me three loaves;
6 For a friend of mine in his journey is come to me, and I have nothing to set before him?
7 And he from within shall answer and say, Trouble me not: the door is now shut, and my children are with me in bed; I cannot rise and give thee.
8 I say unto you, Though he will not rise and give him, because he is his friend, yet because of his importunity he will rise and give him as many as he needeth.
9 And I say unto you, Ask, and it shall be given you; seek, and ye shall find; knock, and it shall be opened unto you.

10 For every one that asketh receiveth; and he that seeketh findeth; and to him that knocketh it shall be opened.

11 If a son shall ask bread of any of you that is a father, will he give him a stone? or if he ask a fish, will he for a fish give him a serpent?

12 Or if he shall ask an egg, will he offer him a scorpion?

13 If ye then, being evil, know how to give good gifts unto your children: how much more shall your heavenly Father give the Holy Spirit to them that ask him?

The Prayer of Importunity

In this account, which deals with the prayer of importunity, many people have had the mistaken idea that Jesus was teaching us to keep on asking in order to get results.

In this parable we see a man who had a guest arrive during the night. He didn't have any bread to set before him, so he went to his neighbor's house and asked for a loaf of bread. The neighbor responded, "I'm already in bed; don't bother me." But when the man kept pleading with him, he finally granted his request.

Jesus was illustrating here that although the neighbor would not get out of bed to give the man bread just because he was a friend, he gave it to him because of his importunity. Jesus was saying *how much more*

our heavenly Father will hear us and grant our requests.

It is the importunity of faith, not the importunity of unbelief, that gets results. We can keep on begging God — importuning all we want — and we never will get an answer if our importuning prayer is in unbelief.

It is the importunity of faith that works: *"Ask, and it shall be given you; seek, and ye shall find; knock, and it shall be opened unto you."*

Andrew Murray had real insight into this subject of importunity in prayer. He said it is not good taste to ask the Lord for the same thing over and over again. He said if the thing which you have prayed about hasn't materialized, don't ask again the same way you did in the beginning. That would be a confession that you didn't believe God the first time.

Just remind God of your request. Remind Him of what He promised. Remind Him you are expecting the answer, and let this importunity be an importunity of faith. It will bring results.

Luke's account of the story is more detailed then Matthew's, and in verse 13, Luke added something. Matthew recorded, *"If ye then, being evil know how to give good gifts unto your children, how much more shall your Father which is in heaven give*

GOOD THINGS to them that ask him?"

Luke enlarges on this by saying, *"If ye then, being evil know how to give good gifts unto your children: how much more shall your heavenly Father give THE HOLY SPIRIT to them that ask him?"* (Although Matthew didn't specifically name the Holy Spirit in this verse, we know that the Holy Spirit is a "good thing.")

I am sure the Holy Spirit had a purpose for inspiring Luke and Matthew to record this as they did. The Holy Spirit, as He inspired Matthew, wanted to stress the good things of life. He wanted us to know that God loves us just as we love our children and want them to have good things. The Holy Spirit inspired Luke to emphasize the spiritual things God has for us.

By asking, seeking, and knocking in faith, we can enjoy the abundant blessings God has for His children.

✳

Memory Text:

"Ask, and it shall be given you; seek and ye shall find; knock, and it shall be opened unto you."

— Matt. 7:7

What Jesus Said About Prayer (Part 3)

Bible Texts: Matthew 21:18-22; Mark 11:12-14,20-24; John 15:7,8

Central Truth: Where the Word of God abides, there faith abides.

In Matthew 21 we come to another passage where Jesus taught on prayer. He actually was talking about faith *and* prayer. You can't very well talk about faith without talking about prayer, nor can you talk about prayer without talking about faith. They go hand in hand.

Pray, Believe, Receive

MATTHEW 21:18-22
18 Now in the morning as he returned into the city, he hungered.
19 And when he saw a fig tree in the way, he came to it, and found nothing thereon, but leaves only, and said unto it, Let no fruit grow on thee henceforward for ever. And presently the fig tree withered away.
20 And when the disciples saw it, they marvelled, saying, How soon is the fig tree withered away!
21 Jesus answered and said unto them, Verily I say unto you, If ye have faith, and doubt not, ye shall not only do this which is done to the fig tree, but also if ye shall say unto this mountain, Be thou removed, and be thou cast into the sea; it shall be done.
22 And all things, whatsoever ye shall ask in prayer, believing, ye shall receive.

Let's look at this same account in Mark's Gospel. This is the only reference to prayer in the Book of Mark, but the writer devoted a great deal of attention to it. Whereas Matthew told the story in five verses, Mark takes nearly twice as many verses to tell the same story.

23

MARK 11:12-14,20-24

12 And on the morrow, when they were come from Bethany, he was hungry:

13 And seeing a fig tree afar off having leaves, he came, if haply he might find any thing thereon: and when he came to it, he found nothing but leaves; for the time of figs was not yet.

14 And Jesus answered and said unto it, No man eat fruit of thee hereafter for ever. And his disciples heard it. . . .

20 And in the morning, as they passed by, they saw the fig tree dried up from the roots.

21 And Peter calling to remembrance saith unto him, Master, behold, the fig tree which thou cursedst is withered away.

22 And Jesus answering saith unto them, Have faith in God.

23 For verily I say unto you, That whosoever shall say unto this mountain, Be thou removed, and be thou cast into the sea; and shall not doubt in his heart, but shall believe that those things which he saith shall come to pass; he shall have whatsoever he saith.

24 Therefore I say unto you, What things soever ye desire, when ye pray, believe that ye receive them, and ye shall have them.

In studying the Bible, it is good to compare the different Gospel writers' accounts of the same incidents in Jesus' life. In this way we get different viewpoints. (One writer may give us details that the others left out.)

In Matthew's account of the above story, Jesus said, *"And all things whatsoever ye shall ask in prayer, believing, ye shall receive"* (v. 22). Mark put it a little differently: *". . . What things soever ye desire, when ye pray, believe that ye receive them and ye shall have them"* (v. 24). Both writers gave the basic formula for faith: Pray, believe, receive.

Someone has asked, "But what if you didn't receive?"

Then you didn't ask believing, did you? The Scripture says if you pray and believe, you shall receive.

"Yes, but maybe it isn't the will of God," people will reply.

The Scripture didn't say anything about that. We are too quick to use this as an excuse for our unbelief. *Jesus said if you ask in prayer, believing, you shall receive!*

"But what if someone asked for ten million oil wells?" someone might ask.

Well, if you have faith for ten million off wells, you will get them. But I doubt seriously you could believe that. Don't ask me to agree with you in prayer for them, because I don't think I could. However, if you can believe that you will receive ten million oil wells, you will get them.

Sometimes I have believed for things that seemed almost as impossible and have received them. Jesus said it, and I believe it: *"What things soever ye desire, when ye pray, believe that ye receive them and ye shall have them."*

The Word of Faith

In John's account of what Jesus said about prayer, not one time does he use the words "faith" or "believe." Let us look at one example:

JOHN 15:7,8
7 If ye abide in me, and my words abide in you, ye shall ask what ye will, and it shall be done unto you.
8 Herein is my Father glorified, that ye bear much fruit; so shall ye be my disciples.

Why was it unnecessary to use the words "faith" or "believe" in this passage of Scripture about prayer? It is because there is no problem with faith if His words abide in you. There is only a lack of faith when the Word doesn't abide in you, because if the Word doesn't abide, something else does. If the Word abides in you, faith abides in you: *"So then faith cometh by hearing, and hearing by the word of God"* (Rom. 10:17).

A person may be giving mental assent to belief in the Word of God. He could stand up, shake his fist, and declare with fervor that he believes in the verbal inspiration of the Bible, that he believes it from cover to cover from Genesis to Revelation — yet never have the Word abiding in him.

Notice that Jesus didn't say, *"If YE abide in me. . . ."* If He had stopped there, we would automatically have it made as born-again Christians, because with the New Birth we do abide in Christ. But the Scripture goes on to say, *". . . and my words abide in you. . . ."*

The Word is called "the word of faith": *"But what saith it? The word is nigh thee, even in thy mouth, and in thy heart: that is, the word of faith, which we preach"* (Rom. 10:8). If this Word abides in you, it will cause faith to spring up in your heart.

The Light of the Word

That is the reason the Psalmist of old said, *"The entrance of thy words giveth light . . ."* (Ps. 119:130). When we know the Word, we are not praying in the dark. We have light.

Again the Psalmist said, *"Thy word is a lamp unto my feet, and a light unto my path"* (Ps. 119:105). We are not walking in the dark. Our pathway is lighted when we have the Word!

If we have a lighted pathway, we can walk in that light. *". . . if we walk in the light, as he is in the light we have fellowship one with another. . ."* (1 John 1:7). This doesn't say a thing about *standing* in the light. It says "walk." God's Word is a light unto the path that we walk.

The Psalmist also prayed: *". . . quicken thou me according to thy word"* (Ps. 119:25). Jesus said, *"If my words abide in you. . . ."* He cannot quicken us according to His Word — although He wants to — unless His words abide in us; unless we walk in the light of the Word.

I heard F. F. Bosworth preach when he was 75 years old and still active in the Lord's work. He said, "I always start every morning by saying, 'Lord, quicken thou me according to thy Word.' "

Then he went on to say what it meant to him to be quickened according to God's Word. He told me how he still was in good health at age 76. For all those years he had trusted God and never had any kind of medication.

Bosworth lived to be 81 years old and was busy in the Lord's work up until the end. In January 1958, he knew the time had come for him to die. He knew in his spirit that the Lord was coming for him.

A close friend of his flew to his bedside in Florida. When he arrived, Brother Bosworth was sitting up in bed. He lifted his hand and praised God, saying, "Brother, this is the day I have waited for all of my life. I am going home."

He had prayed daily, "Lord, quicken thou me according to thy Word," and the Lord quickened him every day until He took him home. Bosworth died without sickness or disease. He just went home to be with the Lord.

God's Word is true whether or not we put it into practice.

Memory Text:
"If ye abide in me, and my words abide in you, ye shall ask what ye will and it shall be done unto you."
— John 15:7

What Jesus Said About Prayer (Part 4)

Bible Texts: John 14:10-14; 16:23,24,7-11

Central Truth: Whatever our need may be, it is our privilege in Christ to demand that this need be met.

Let us look again into the Gospel of John to see what Jesus had to say about prayer.

As strange as it may seem, John did not record anything the other Gospel writers did in regard to prayer. The others did not include what he wrote in their accounts. John said if everything Jesus said and did was written, the world itself could not contain the books. He said he wrote that we might believe that Jesus is the Son of God.

Not all the Gospel writers recorded the same thing. Luke recorded part of what Matthew said. Mark recorded only one instance of Jesus teaching on prayer, as we saw in our last lesson on Mark 11:12-24, the cursing of the fig tree. Matthew covered this in Matthew 21.

Matthew also talked about the prayer of agreement, which none of the other writers mentioned: *". . . if two of you shall agree on earth as touching any thing that they shall ask, it shall be done for them of my Father which is in heaven"* (Matt. 18:19). Actually, we have to put all the accounts together to get a clear picture of Jesus' teachings on prayer.

John covers the subject of prayer from an entirely different standpoint. Let us look at two passages of Scripture which seem similar, but really are quite different.

JOHN 14:10-14

10 Believest thou not that I am in the Father, and the Father in me? the words that I speak unto you I speak not of myself: but the Father

that dwelleth in me, he doeth the works.

11 Believe me that I am in the Father, and the Father in me: or else believe me for the very works' sake.

12 Verily, verily, I say unto you, He that believeth on me, the works that I do shall he do also; and greater works than these shall he do; because I go unto my Father.

13 And whatsoever ye shall ask in my name, that will I do, that the Father may be glorified in the Son.

14 If ye shall ask any thing in my name, I will do it.

Many think this scripture refers to prayer, but Jesus is not talking about prayer here at all.

Now let us compare two verses in John 16.

JOHN 16:23,24

23 And in that day ye shall ask me nothing. Verily, verily, I say unto you, Whatsoever ye shall ask the Father in my name, he will give it you.

24 Hitherto have ye asked nothing in name: ask, and ye shall receive, that your joy may be full.

In this passage of Scripture, Jesus was talking about something entirely different from what He was talking about in chapter 14. In John chapter 16 He said, *"Whatsoever ye shall ask the Father in my name, HE will give it you."* But in John 14 He says, *"And whatsoever ye shall ask in my name, that will I do. . . ."* He is talking about two different things.

To Demand As Our Right

Let us examine these scriptures in the Greek New Testament. The Greek word here translated "ask" means "demand." Or, "Whatsoever ye shall *demand* in my name, that will I do."

We are not demanding it of God. When we pray, we ask of God in Jesus Name. But we are demanding this of the devil.

Actually, the Greek is more explicit than the English translation. The Greek reads, "Whatsoever ye shall demand as your right . . ." (not ask as a favor).

Whatever we ask or demand as our right, Jesus said, "I will do it." We have the right to demand that Satan take his hands off our finances if we are having difficulty making ends meet. Whatever our need may be, it is our privilege, our right, in Christ to ask, to demand, that this need be met.

We see an example of this in the Book of Acts. Peter and John saw a crippled man begging alms at the gate called Beautiful. Peter stopped and said, "Look on us." The man looked at them, expecting to receive a coin. Peter said, *"Silver and gold* have I none; but such as I have give I thee: In the name of Jesus Christ of Nazareth rise up and walk" (Acts 3:6).

Peter demanded in Jesus' Name that the cripple get up and walk. He didn't pray that God would do it. He knew Jesus had said that whatever we demand, or ask, in His name, He would do.

Just before Jesus said, "Whatsoever ye shall ask [demand] in my name, that will I do," He said, "He that believeth on me, the works that I do shall he do also. . . ." Peter was doing the works Jesus did when he healed the cripple.

Even though we pray for the sick today — and this is certainly scriptural (James 5:14-16) — Jesus never prayed for the sick.

Jesus said, ". . . the works that I do shall he do also. . . ." If we just prayed for the sick and got results, we wouldn't be doing the works Jesus did. Jesus laid hands on the sick, but He never prayed for them He would command the devil to leave, or He would just say, "Go thy way, and as thou hast believed, so be it done unto thee" (Matt. 8:13).

So when Jesus said in John 14:13, "And whatsoever ye shall ask [demand] in my name, that will I do," He was not talking about praying to

God the Father; He was talking about doing the same works He did.

Greater Works

Not only did Jesus say that we would do the *same* works that He did; He also said, ". . . *and GREATER works than these shall he do . . .*" (John 14:12). Then He went on to tell us *why* we would do greater works: ". . . *because I go unto my Father.*" The greater works that the Church can do and is doing today are due to the fact that Jesus has gone to the Father.

JOHN 16:7-11
7 Nevertheless I tell you the truth; It is expedient [profitable, for your best] for you that I go away: for if I go not away, the Comforter will not come unto you; but if I depart, I will send him unto you.
8 And when he is come, he will reprove the world of sin, and of righteousness, and of judgment:
9 Of sin, because they believe not on me;
10 Of righteousness, because I go to my Father, and ye see me no more;
11 Of judgment, because the prince of this world is judged.

What are these greater works? We show men and women how to become born again. "But weren't people saved, or born again, under Jesus' ministry?" someone might ask. They were saved in the same sense that the people in the Old Testament were saved, but they were not "born again." The work of the Holy Spirit is necessary in the New Birth, and while Jesus was on earth the Holy Spirit had not yet been given. This is why Jesus said, ". . . *It is expedient for you that I go away: for if I go not away, the Comforter will not come unto you; but if I depart, I will send him unto you"* (John 16:7).

"But didn't Jesus forgive people's sins while He was here on earth?" someone might say. Yes, but there is a difference between having one's sins forgiven and being born again.

After a person is born again, if he sins, he can get forgiveness, but he is not born again a second time. (If that were true, we might be born again thousands of times.) The New Birth is a greater work than a healing or a miracle.

So people were not born again while Jesus was on earth. Second, we never read in the four Gospels, *"And the Lord added daily to the Church such as should be saved."* However, we do see this repeatedly in the Book of Acts. This is because there *wasn't* any Church in Jesus' day in the sense that we think of the New Testament Church.

The only Body of Christ that was on earth was His *physical* body.

There were those who believed on Him and who had the promise of that which was to come, but their beliefs could only be consummated when the Holy Spirit came to baptize them all into one Body. The Body had to be formed.

Today we are the spiritual Body of Christ. The only Body of Christ in the world today is the Church.

Not only was no one born again or added to the Church under the ministry of Jesus, neither was anyone filled with the Holy Spirit under His ministry. These are "the greater works" that we do because He went to the Father.

Praying in Jesus' Name

Let us compare now what Jesus said in John 16 regarding prayer: *"And in that day ye shall ask me nothing . . ."* (v. 23). When He said "in that day," He was referring to the day in which we now live — the day of the New Covenant, the day of the New Testament.

One translation of this verse reads, "In that day ye shall not pray to me." He told us not to pray to Him, but to pray to the Father in Jesus' Name. ". . . *Whatsoever ye shall ask the Father in my name, he will give it you."*

Then He went on to say, *"Hitherto have ye asked nothing in my name:*

ask, and ye shall receive, that your joy may be full" (v. 24).

He was telling His disciples that while He was on the earth with them, they did not pray to the Father in Jesus' Name; however, "in that day," when He would no longer be on the earth, they would ask the Father in the Name of Jesus, *"and ye shall receive, that your joy may be full."*

Our heavenly Father longs to meet our every need — if only we would ask Him — so our joy may be full!

✳

Memory Text:

"If ye shall ask any thing in my name, I will do it."

— John 14:14

What Paul Said About Prayer (Part 1)

Bible Text: 1 Thessalonians 5:16-18

Central Truth: When we are fully trusting God, we can thank Him in every circumstance of life.

In his writings to the Early Church, Paul had much to say to these new Christians about prayer. In the next two lessons, we will merely look at *some* of the things he had to say about prayer.

1 THESSALONIANS 5:16-18
16 Rejoice evermore.
17 Pray without ceasing.
18 In every thing give thanks: for this is the will of God in Christ Jesus concerning you.

Verse 17 in the *King James Version* is a little misleading. Some people have gotten the idea that Paul was telling us here to pray all the time. Other translations of this verse read, "Never give up in prayer," or "Be unceasing in prayer." In other words, don't give up your prayer life.

Maintain a prayer life. It doesn't mean that we are to pray with every breath. This is not possible.

The exhortation never to give up in prayer is sandwiched between the exhortations to "rejoice" and "give thanks." That is a good "sandwich," isn't it? Paul said, "Rejoice evermore." We are to be full of rejoicing.

Then he said, *"In every thing give thanks: for this is the will of God in Christ Jesus concerning you."*

"But I just can't thank God in *everything!*" some might exclaim.

Paul said you could. He said this is the will of God in Christ Jesus concerning *you.* We all want to be in the will of God. And we can when we have things in their proper perspective.

When we know and act upon the Word of God, we can truly thank Him in everything. I have done this in my own life when things looked bleak.

When I first started out on the evangelistic field, often I would close one revival meeting with no other meetings in sight.

I had a wife and two children to support. At the time, my niece also was living with us, so there were five of us to feed and clothe.

When I would close a revival and put the last offering in my pocket, often it wouldn't be enough to pay the rent when I got home. I wouldn't have enough money to buy food. And I didn't have any prospects for other meetings.

On one such occasion I started driving home at night after the closing service. I drove then because my tires were bald, and I had a better chance of making it at night when it was cooler. (During the daytime, the roads were hot, and there was a greater risk of a blowout. And I didn't even have a spare tire.)

All the way home, the devil perched on my shoulder and whispered in my ear, "What are you going to do now? What are you going to do now?" I didn't have air-conditioning, so the windows were rolled down. I could hear the tires singing, and it

seemed as if they picked up the phrase and taunted me: "What are you going to do now? What are you going to do now?" It kept getting louder and louder.

But thank God when you have the Word, you can walk in the light of the Word.

I said, "I'll tell you what I am going to do, Mr. Devil: I'm going to act just as if the Word of God is so. The Bible says, 'Rejoice evermore.' I rejoice for the $42 offering I did get. The Bible says, 'In every thing give thanks . . .' I thank God for the $42. I may have needed $102, but I thank God for the $42. I am rejoicing. I am giving thanks.

"And I'll tell you something else, Mr. Devil. I thank God for this test, for this is a good time to prove that God and the Bible are true. This is an opportunity for me to believe God, and I am thanking Him for it. Since you asked me what I'm going to do, I'll tell you exactly what I'm going to do: I'm going to go home, go to bed, and sleep like a baby."

I arrived home around two o'clock in the morning, and my wife asked, "How did everything go?" I knew she was wondering if I had received enough money to meet the bills.

"Everything is just fine," I told her. "We don't have a thing in the world to worry about. I'll tell you about it in the morning." Then I went to bed and slept soundly and peacefully.

Early the next morning, before I had awakened, the phone rang. When Oretha handed it to me, I found that the caller was a pastor I had heard of but hadn't actually met.

He asked, "When can you start a meeting with us?"

"As soon as you want me to," I answered.

"Then how about starting next Sunday?" he said.

"I'll be there," I said, praising God in my heart for answered prayer, for meeting my needs again as He had in the past because I had trusted in Him.

I had obeyed God's Word and had rejoiced in the face of despair. If I had griped all the way home, I am not sure it would have worked out that way.

✳

Memory Text:

"In every thing give thanks: for this is the will of God in Christ Jesus concerning you."

— 1 Thess. 5:18

What Paul Said About Prayer (Part 2)

Bible Texts: 1 Timothy 2:1,2,8; 4:1-5

Central Truth: Prayer, accompanied by obedient surrender to God, touches heaven.

In Paul's writings to the young minister Timothy, he had a number of instructions regarding prayer. At this time Timothy was the pastor of a New Testament church.

Pray for Heads of Government

1 TIMOTHY 2:1,2

1 I exhort therefore, that, first of all, supplications, prayers, intercessions, and giving of thanks, be made for all men;

2 For kings, and for all that are in authority; that we may lead a quiet and peaceable life in all godliness and honesty.

Too often we put ourselves first in our praying. In fact, sometimes that is as far as we ever get — just praying for ourselves and our own personal lives and needs.

But here Paul instructed Timothy, "... *FIRST OF ALL, supplications, prayers, intercessions, and giving of thanks, be made for all men.*" Then he became more specific and said, "*For kings, and for all that are in authority. . . .*" (In that day, people were ruled by kings. This would be comparable to presidents and other heads of government in our day.)

Why did Paul say we should pray for those in authority? "... *that we may lead a quiet and peaceable life in all godliness and honesty.*" Whatever happens in the nation we live in affects all of us. God is concerned about us, and whether or not our leaders are Christians, God will do some things for our sake.

We notice that intercession is mentioned here. When Abraham

interceded for Sodom and Gomorrah, God came down and talked with him before destroying those wicked cities. Abraham pleaded with God not to destroy the cities if as many as ten righteous people could be found, and God said, *"I will not destroy it for ten's sake"* (Gen. 18:32).

There are more than ten righteous people in the United States, so we need not be frightened, but we do need to intercede for our country and the heads of government. God will do some things just because we ask Him.

Pray With Hands Outstretched to Heaven

1 TIMOTHY 2:8
8 I will therefore that men pray every where, lifting up holy hands, without wrath and doubting.

Everyone will agree with the first part of Paul's statement to Timothy — that men everywhere ought to pray. But notice Paul also gives some explicit instructions on prayer: *". . . lifting up holy hands, without wrath and doubting."*

We would all encourage people to pray without doubting. Jesus said, *". . . whosoever shall say unto this mountain, Be thou removed, and be thou cast into the sea; and SHALL NOT DOUBT in his heart, but shall believe that those things which he* saith shall come to pass; he shall have whatsoever he saith"* (Mark 11:23). (Certainly we also can see the necessity of praying without wrath.)

If we encourage people to follow two-thirds of Paul's instructions in this verse, then we also should obey his third admonition: *". . . lifting UP holy hands. . . ."*

Those of us who come from denominational churches may find it difficult at first to lift our hands in prayer. I can remember when I first came around people who lifted their hands to pray. It was the hardest thing I had ever done in my life to lift my hands and pray.

Someone may ask, "Do you *have* to do it?" No, you don't *have* to do it, but if we are going to obey part of the verse, why not *all* of it? Why not pray New Testament style?

If Paul was writing to the Church under the inspiration of the Spirit of God, I am under obligation to obey. If *part* of it is inspired of God, then *all* of it is inspired, and we need to pay attention to it.

Sanctifying Prayer

1 TIMOTHY 4:1-5
1 Now the Spirit speaketh expressly, that in the latter times some shall depart from the faith, giving heed to seducing spirits, and doctrines of devils;

2 Speaking lies in hypocrisy, having their conscience seared with a hot iron;
3 Forbidding to marry, and commanding to abstain from meats, which God hath created to be received with thanksgiving of them which believe and know the truth.
4 And every creature of God is good, and nothing to be refused, if it be received with thanksgiving;
5 For it is sanctified by the word of God and prayer.

In this passage, Paul is not referring to sinners or the heathen world. He is talking about believers who depart from the faith. Verse one says that *". . . some shall depart from the faith, giving heed to seducing spirits, and doctrines of devils."*

Then in verse three he mentions some of these doctrines of devils: *"Forbidding to marry, and commanding to abstain from meats . . ."* Most of us have met individuals who have fallen prey to such erroneous teaching.

But Paul, speaking under the inspiration of the Holy Spirit, said concerning meats, *". . . which God hath created to be received with thanksgiving to them which believe and know the truth. And every creature of God is good, and nothing to be refused, if it be received with thanksgiving: For it is sanctified by the word of God and prayer."*

The devil will use any means he can to lead people away from God.

I once knew a minister who was on fire for God and had a remarkable ministry in reaching the lost. He could get more people saved accidentally than most people can on purpose.

But he got off on the subject of diet, and he started teaching people what to eat and what not to eat. He preached Old Testament dietary laws and spent all his time trying to regulate people's diets. If he got anyone saved, I don't know of it. The devil undermined his ministry of reaching the lost.

People have asked me, "Do you eat pork?" Certainly I eat pork. I sanctify it *"by the word of God and prayer,"* as Paul teaches. You could eat skunk if you wanted to, because *". . . every creature of God is good, and nothing to be refused, if it be received with thanksgiving"* (v. 4).

We can regulate our diet however we want as long as we receive it with thanksgiving and it is sanctified with prayer. Then nothing we eat need hurt us. Nothing I eat ever hurts me, because I sanctify it. So many people tell me they can't eat this or they can't eat that because it hurts them if they do. It need not, if you will sanctify it as Paul teaches us in this passage of Scripture.

We need to be careful of segments of the church world which have gone off into these areas, because Paul says that they have given *"heed to seducing spirits, and doctrines of devils."*

---

*

Memory Text:

"I will therefore that men pray every where, lifting up holy hands, without wrath and doubting."

— 1 Tim. 2:8

What Others Said About Prayer (Part 1)

Bible Texts: James 5:13-18; Jude 20,21

Central Truth: Our prayers are not answered on the basis of how good we have been, but on the basis of our right standing in Christ.

Now let's turn to some other writers and see what they have to say on the subject of prayer.

What James Said About Prayer

JAMES 5:13-16

13 Is any among you afflicted? let him pray. Is any merry? let him sing psalms.

14 Is any sick among you? let him call for the elders of the church; and let them pray over him, anointing him with oil in the name of the Lord:

15 And the prayer of faith shall save the sick, and the Lord shall raise him up; and if he have committed sins, they shall forgiven him.

16 Confess your faults one to another, and pray one for another, that ye may be healed. The effectual fervent prayer of a righteous man availeth much.

James asks three questions: "Is any among you afflicted? Is any merry? Is any sick among you?" He is talking about three different things here. The words "afflicted" and "sick" do not mean the same thing in this verse of Scripture. James gave one instruction for the afflicted and another instruction for those who were sick.

The Greek word translated here "afflicted" doesn't refer to illness or physical affliction. It means a test or trial. James said if you are going through a test or trial, do your own praying. Not many people do that. Most people run around looking for someone else to do their praying for them. But James didn't say a word about getting anyone to pray for you in this situation. He said, *"let him pray."*

This doesn't mean it's not all right for us to pray for one another. The main thing God wants us to learn is to do our own praying, because we then gain great victories. If you have to depend on someone else to pray you out of a trial, then the next time you are confronted with one of life's tests, you still won't know the way out. You still will have to find someone else to pray you out, and if you can't find someone, you might not make it.

James said, *"Is any merry? let him sing psalms."* This passage of Scripture needs little comment. It's easy to sing when we are merry, isn't it?

James then said, "Is any sick among you? let him call for the elders of the church, and let them pray over him. . . ." P. C. Nelson, who was a Greek scholar, brought out in his writing that the Greek word translated "sick" implies that the person is so ill he can't do anything for himself. He is helpless.

If a person had a headache or some minor ailment, he could go to the church, where the pastor could pray for him. But when he is so ill he can't get out of bed, he is to call for the elders of the church to pray for him.

(We must remember that when James wrote his epistle, the Church was in her infancy. The disciples would go to a place where there wasn't a church, preach, win people to the Lord, and establish a work. These new churches didn't have all the ministry gifts. Because some churches didn't have a pastor, they would appoint the eldest in the con-gregation, or in some places they would appoint those who had matured most spiritually to be in charge and watch over the flock. As the church developed and grew, God gave *". . . some, apostles; and some, prophets; and some, evangelists; and some, pastors and teachers"* (Eph. 4:11). So in the process of time, there were those who were separated unto the ministry.)

Can a Person With Sin in His Life Be Healed?

James instructed those who were sick to call for the elders to pray for them and anoint them with oil. *"And the prayer of faith shall save the sick, and the Lord shall raise him up; and if he have committed sins, they shall be forgiven him"* (James 5:15). James wasn't saying that everyone is ill because of having committed sins; he was saying the reason *some* are sick is because they have sinned: *"If he have committed sins, they shall be forgiven him."* There is forgiveness and healing for us.

Many people think because they have failed God they must continue to be sick because they must "pay" for their sins. However, this scripture doesn't say, "If he have committed sins, he has to go on being sick to pay for them." It says, *"If he have committed sins, THEY SHALL BE FORGIVEN HIM."*

James went on to say, *"Confess your faults one to another, and pray one for another, that ye may be healed"* (v.16). This is all tied together. We can't take this verse out of its setting and apply it incorrectly. James wasn't suggesting that we come to church to have a confession meeting. He was saying that when the elders come to pray for the sick man, if he has sinned, he should confess his sin. He isn't going to get healed with unconfessed sin in his life!

What Is a 'Righteous' Man?

James followed this admonition with the words, *"The effectual fervent prayer of a righteous man availeth much."* Then in the next two verses he gave us an example of a righteous man.

JAMES 5:17,18
17 Elias [Elijah] was a man subject to like passions as we are, and he prayed earnestly that it might not rain: and it rained not on the earth by the space of three years and six months.
18 And he prayed again, and the heaven gave rain, and the earth brought forth her fruit.

You might think, as I once did, *But Elijah was a prophet. He was a great man of God. I can't possibly do what he did.* However, James didn't say, "Elijah was a prophet, and he prayed." He said Elijah was a man *"subject to like passions as we are."* He had the same faults and failings we do, and he made the same mistakes — yet his prayers worked.

God doesn't hear a prophet more quickly than He hears any other believer. James didn't say it was the "effectual fervent prayer of a prophet" that got the job done. He said, *"The effectual fervent prayer of a righteous man. . . ."*

"Well, if I were righteous I could do it," you might say. But you are righteous if you are saved, because you are the *"righteousness of God in him* [Christ]*"* (2 Cor. 5:21). God made you righteous; you can't make yourself righteous.

As a pastor for nearly 12 years, I often saw people in my congregation who didn't live half as consecrated lives as others did, yet they could pray twice as effectively as the others. They could pray the prayer of faith more quickly for themselves and their families. I was puzzled about this until the Lord finally showed me through His Word that we don't get our prayers answered on the basis of how good or how bad we have been; it is on the basis of our right standing in Him.

We are made righteous in Christ Jesus. *"For he hath made him to be sin for us, who knew no sin; that we might be made the righteousness of God in him"* (2 Cor. 5:21).

Righteousness means right standing with God. Jesus is our righteousness. Every one of us who is a born-again believer has the same right standing or righteousness Jesus has. We are invited to come boldly to the throne of grace by way of the blood of Jesus.

What Jude Said About Prayer

Jude also said something about prayer that is enlightening and helpful.

JUDE 20,21
20 But ye, beloved, building up yourselves on your most holy faith, praying in the Holy Ghost.
21 Keep yourselves in the love of God, looking for the mercy of our Lord Jesus Christ unto eternal life.

Jude's teachings here agree with what Paul said to the Church at Corinth: *"For if I pray in an unknown tongue, my spirit prayeth . . . ,"* and *"He that speaketh in an unknown tongue edifieth himself . . ."* (1 Cor. 14:14,4).

The word "edify" means to build up. Praying in an unknown tongue edifies or builds up the believer. You could say it is a means of "spiritual muscle building."

Jude didn't say praying in the Holy Spirit would build up your faith. He said, *". . . building up yourselves on your most holy faith. . . ."*

It's foolish to take a text out of its setting and try to prove something with it. We shouldn't try to make a verse say something that doesn't agree with the rest of the passage. We must interpret the verse in the light of the whole passage. We must study it in context, putting all the verses together. Then one verse will help and modify the other and they will fit together.

Romans 10:17 tells us how to build up our faith. *"So then faith cometh by hearing, and hearing by the word of God."* We build up our faith through the study of God's Word. Then, through praying in tongues, we build up ourselves spiritually on the faith we already have.

We can build spiritual muscle tone into our everyday lives as we are edified through praying in the Spirit.

✳

Memory Text:

". . . The effectual fervent prayer of a righteous man availeth much."

— James 5:16

What Others Said About Prayer (Part 2)

Bible Texts: 1 Peter 3:1-6,12; 1 John 5:14-16; Hebrews 6:4-6; 10:26-29; 3 John 2

Central Truth: God's eyes and ears are ever open to the cries of the righteous.

In Peter's epistles to the Church, he, too, gave believers instructions in the matter of prayer.

Relationship to Spouse Can Hinder Prayers

"Likewise, ye husbands, dwell with them according to knowledge, giving honour unto the wife, as unto the weaker vessel, and as being heirs together of the grace of life; THAT YOUR PRAYERS BE NOT HINDERED" (1 Peter 3:7). Peter is talking about marriages in which both husband and wife are believers, because he said, *". . . being heirs together of the grace of life. . . ."*

Men, if some of your prayers are not being answered, perhaps you should examine your relationship with your wife. Do you show her tenderness and respect, *"giving honour unto the wife, as unto the weaker vessel"?* If not, Peter says that your prayers are hindered.

He gives similar admonitions to wives. Let us look at them.

1 PETER 3:1-6

1 Likewise, ye wives, be in subjection to your own husbands; that, if any obey not the word, they also may without the word be won by the conversation of the wives;

2 While they behold your chaste conversation coupled with fear.

3 Whose adorning let it not be that outward adorning of plaiting of the hair, and of wearing of gold, or of putting on of apparel;

4 But let it be the hidden man of the heart, in that which is not corruptible, even the ornament of a

45

meek and quiet spirit, which is in the sight of God of great price.

5 For after this manner in the old time the holy women also, who trusted in God, adorned themselves, being in subjection unto their own husbands:

6 Even as Sara obeyed Abraham, calling him lord: whose daughters ye are, as long as ye do well, and are not afraid with any amazement.

Here Peter suggests that there is a way of winning an unsaved husband without the Word: *". . . if any obey not the word, they also may without the word be won by the conversation of the wives."* The word "conversation" here means one's manner of life; her conduct.

God Hears Prayers of Righteous

Further on in this chapter, Peter has more to say about prayer.

1 PETER 3:12

12 For the eyes of the Lord are over the righteous, and his ears are open unto their prayers: but the face of the Lord is against them that do evil.

Who are the righteous that this verse refers to? In Lesson 9 we saw that we, as born-again believers, are the righteous in Christ Jesus: *"For he hath made him to be sin for us, who knew no sin; that we might be*

made the righteousness of God in him" (2 Cor. 5:21). Righteousness is not based on how good or bad we are, but on our standing in Christ. Jesus is our righteousness.

Peter said that God's eyes are over us, and *". . . his ears are open unto* [our] *prayers. . . ."* I'm glad God has eyes and ears, aren't you? He sees us and He hears us. His ears are open to our prayers; but as we saw in verse seven, we can hinder our prayers. God doesn't hinder them — He doesn't refuse to hear — but we can hinder them. Let us take care that we don't hinder them; then we can know His ears are open unto our prayers.

Watch and Pray

Then in First Peter 4:7 we read, *"But the end of all things is at hand, be ye therefore sober, and watch unto prayer."* Under the inspiration of the Holy Spirit, Peter saw into the future to the day in which we live and admonished believers concerning the necessity of watchful prayer. In Mark's Gospel we read where Jesus, talking about the last days, said *"Take ye heed, watch and pray: for ye know not when the time is"* (Mark 13:33).

God's Will in Prayer

John, too, had important things to say about prayer.

1 JOHN 5:14-16

14 And this is the confidence that we have in him, that, if we ask any thing according to his will, he heareth us:

15 And if we know that he hear us, whatsoever we ask, we know that we have the petitions that we desired of him.

16 If any man see his brother sin a sin which is not unto death, he shall ask, and he shall give him life for them that sin not unto death. There is a sin unto death: I do not say that he shall pray for it.

Although the word "pray" is mentioned only once in this passage of Scripture, John has used the words "ask" and "petition," referring to prayer. He said, ". . . *if we ask any thing according to his will he heareth us.*" Remember this: If it is according to the Word, it is according to His will.

Some people take the attitude that they will pray for something and if it is God's will, He will give it to them. If it isn't His will, then He won't. However, this isn't what the Bible says.

John said, "*. . . if we ask any thing according to his will he heareth us.*" His Word is His Will. If we know what His Word says about a certain matter, then we know what His will is about that matter. This agrees with Jesus' statement, "*. . . if ye abide*

in me, and my words abide in you, ye shall ask what ye will and it shall be done unto you" (John 15:7).

Verse 16 of the above passage has been the subject of much controversy, and most preachers just stay away from it. However, it ties right in with the two preceding verses and continues talking about prayer:

1 JOHN 5:16

16 If any man see his brother sin a sin which is not unto death, he shall ask, and he shall give him life for them that sin not unto death. There is a sin unto death: I do not say that he shall pray for it.

John is saying here that if we ask God to forgive someone, this is according to His Word and according to His will, and He will do it.

Some years ago, I was holding a meeting near my hometown in Texas when I received a call that my grandmother had fallen into a coma and was near death at her home. Each night after the evening service I drove back to her home and would sit up with her through the night. She never regained consciousness.

The third night as I sat there I prayed, "Dear Lord, I'm so sorry I didn't pray with Granny the other day when I visited her."

I knew Granny was a Christian and loved the Lord, but there are sins of omission as well as commission and I could see where she had missed it. (Others can see where I have missed it. We can see where others miss it sometimes better than we can see ourselves.)

So I prayed, "Lord, I wish I had prayed with her. Just let her revive so I can have a word of prayer with her. (She was elderly and I knew in my spirit she was going to go.) Let me make sure there isn't any unconfessed sin in her life."

As I prayed, Someone said, "Why don't you ask Me to forgive her?"

It was so real it startled me. I jumped out of the chair and the Bible on my lap scooted across the floor and under the bed.

"Who said that?" I asked. I thought someone had heard me praying and was teasing me. However, I found no one when I looked around the room and outside the door. I sat back down and began to study, but I couldn't concentrate, so I started to pray again.

"Lord, why don't you bring her out of it and let me have a word of prayer with her to see that she doesn't die with any unconfessed sin in her life?"

Again that Voice said, "Why don't you ask Me to forgive her?"

I jumped again and said, "Someone is playing tricks on me." But a check into the bedrooms of everyone else in the house revealed that they were sound asleep.

I went back to Granny's bedroom and tried to study, but I could not, so I began to pray again.

When I did, He said the third time, "Why don't you ask Me to forgive her?"

This time I had the presence of mind to remember that Eli had told the child Samuel to answer when God called. I realized it was the Lord, and I answered, "Me ask You?"

He said, "Yes, you ask Me. Don't you know that my Word says in First John 5:16, *'If any man see his brother sin a sin which is not unto death, he shall ask, and he shall give him life for them . . .'?"*

I turned the pages of my Bible to that scripture and read it. "That's right. That's exactly what it says! All right, Lord, I ask You. Please forgive her. You can forgive her of these things that I can see of omission, and of anything else that she didn't see or I don't see, You forgive her."

He said, "All right, I have."

I thanked Him for it. To me that settled it. Can't you see that this was according to His will?

The last part of that verse does make an exception, however. It says, *". . . there is a sin unto death: I do not say that he shall pray for it."* How will we know if a person has committed this sin unto death? *We will only know this as the Holy Spirit reveals it to us.*

This has happened to me only two times in my life when I have been praying for someone and the Lord showed me that there was no need to pray for them, because they had sinned the sin unto death.

What is this sin unto death? First, John is not talking about *physical* death here, but about *spiritual* death. This isn't a sin that an unbeliever can commit. It is a sin only a Christian can commit, for he used the term "brother."

Let us look into the Book of Hebrews to find out more about this.

HEBREWS 6:4-6
4 For it is impossible for those who were once enlightened, and have tasted of the heavenly gift, and were made partakers of the Holy Ghost,
5 And have tasted the good word of God, and the powers of the world to come,
6 If they shall fall away, to renew them again unto repentance; seeing they crucify to themselves the Son of God afresh, and put him to an open shame.

HEBREWS 10:26-29
26 For if we sin wilfully after that we have received the knowledge of the truth, there remaineth no more sacrifice for sins,
27 But a certain fearful looking for of judgment and fiery indignation, which shall devour the adversaries.
28 He that despised Moses' law died without mercy under two or three witnesses:
29 Of how much sorer punishment, suppose ye, shall he be thought worthy, who hath trodden under foot the Son of God, and hath counted the blood of the covenant, wherewith he was sanctified, an unholy thing, and hath done despite unto the Spirit of grace?

The sin God is talking about here is not the sin of lying, cheating, or something like that. God offers forgiveness for such sins. There is no forgiveness, however, for those who have *"trodden under foot the Son of God. . . ."*

The Hebrew Christians to whom this book was written were under great persecution and were tempted to go back to Judaism. When they accepted Christ, they were cut off from their families, ran into financial hardships, and faced numerous other trials. But God warned them in these scriptures that to go back to Judaism was to deny Christ. It was to say that they would be counting "the blood of the covenant, wherewith he was sanctified, an unholy thing," or, in other words, that Jesus' blood was just common blood like any other man's.

Let us remember that as long as a person stays in Christ, he is eternally secure. But we don't want to forget that there is a sin unto death.

John's Three-Dimensional Prayer

3 JOHN 2

2 Beloved, I wish above all things that thou mayest prosper and be in health, even as thy soul prospereth.

Memory Text:

"For the eyes of the Lord are over the righteous, and his ears are open unto their prayers: but the face of the Lord is against them that do evil."

— 1 Peter 3:12

The word translated "wish" in the *King James Version* is "pray" in the original Greek. Therefore, John said here, *"Beloved, I PRAY above all things that thou mayest prosper and be in health, even as thy soul prospereth."* If he was motivated by the Spirit to pray that way, that would be the desire of the Spirit of God for every person. It is all right, then, to pray for financial prosperity, because John said, *"I pray above all things. . . ."*

John's prayer here concerns three dimensions of our lives: physical, spiritual, and material. He said, *". . . I pray . . . that thou mayest prosper* [material blessing] *and be in health* [physical blessing], *even as thy soul prospereth* [spiritual blessing]." Thus, we see that God desires to bless every part of the believer's life.

50

The Will of God
In Prayer
(Part 1)

Bible Texts: John 3:16; 2 Peter 3:9; Acts 16:31

Central Truth: If our prayer request is according to God's Word, it is according to His will.

In the next three lessons we will focus our attention on the will of God in prayer.

As we look at our memory text, First John 5:14, notice the words "confidence" and "heareth": *"And this is the CONFIDENCE that we have in him, that if we ask any thing according to his will he HEARETH us."* Another translation of this verse says, "And this is the boldness we have toward him. . . ."

Under what condition can we have confidence that God hears us when we pray? He hears us if we ask anything according to His will!

In the next verse we read, *"And if we know that he hear us, whatsoever we ask, we know that we have the petitions that we desired of him."* Notice that this scripture says, *"And if . . . he hear us . . . we have the peti-*

tions that we desired. . . ." It would seem from reading this that there must be something He *doesn't* hear.

If we don't have this confidence or boldness when we pray, it must mean that the Lord doesn't hear us. If we don't fulfill our part, it won't work.

How can we get confidence, boldness, and faith? The Word of God gives faith: *"So then faith cometh by hearing, and hearing by the word of God"* (Rom. 10:17). *"The entrance of thy words giveth light . . ."* (Ps. 119:130). *"Thy word is a lamp unto my feet and a light unto my path"* (Ps. 119:105). When we walk in the light of the Word, we are not walking in darkness.

Many times we pray in darkness because we don't know what God's will is. We don't come with confidence or boldness. We come trembling and fearful, hoping He will hear us, but that won't work.

We first need to go to God's Word and find out what it says about our particular problem. Then we can pray in faith, knowing His will in the matter. (Almost everything we need to pray about is covered in His Word.)

The Will of God Concerning Salvation

First of all, we know that saving the lost is God's will, because that is why Jesus came to earth and died.

JOHN 3:16
16 For God so loved the world, that he gave his only begotten Son, that whosoever believeth in him should not perish, but have everlasting life.

2 PETER 3:9
9 The Lord is not slack concerning his promise, as some men count slackness; but is longsuffering to usward, not willing that any should perish, but that all should come to repentance.

ACTS 16:31
31 And they said, Believe on the Lord Jesus Christ, and thou shalt be saved, and thy house.

I don't know of anyone who would pray for a lost loved one by saying, "Lord, *if it is your will* save him."

However, much of our praying for the lost is not effective. Why? Because we do not come with confidence and boldness.

Our text says if we come with confidence and boldness, asking according to His will, we know that God hears us and we have the petitions we desire. That should be clear enough. However, our praying is too often, in the natural realm rather than in the spiritual realm. We pray, "God save our loved one," and then we wait to see if God has answered our prayer! If the person gets saved immediately, we believe God heard us. If he doesn't — if we see no change in his life — we think God didn't hear us. This is walking by sight, not by faith, and it brings only confusion.

You might say, "I have prayed and prayed for my unsaved loved ones, and it seems as if my praying doesn't work." Return to God's Word and you'll discover why your prayers aren't answered: *"And this is the confidence that we have in him, that, if we ask any thing according to his will. . . ."*

There's no question that it's God's will to save the lost, as we just saw from the Scriptures. The Word of God is the will of God. Therefore, if our request is in accordance with His will, we know we have the petitions we desire of Him.

I once knew a country preacher who, because of his limited education, never had an opportunity to pastor a large church. Most of his pastorates were small community churches. However, he was in constant demand to hold revivals because of his tremendous soul-winning. Wherever he went, a landslide of souls resulted. He could go to a church where no one had been saved in years, and great numbers would accept Christ as Savior.

When he was in his early sixties and still enjoying phenomenal success, I once asked him the secret of his success.

"It is a very simple thing," he told me. "I just apply the same faith to see folks saved as I do to see them healed or to believe God for anything else. It never enters my mind to doubt that people will come to be saved. If doubt did come, I would resist it in the Name of Jesus.

"I pray, but not more than others do. I do seek God, of course, but I attribute my success in soul-winning to one thing: *I have confidence the unsaved will come.* By the eye of faith I see the altar filling up with lost souls. And if the meeting doesn't go as well as it should, I don't necessarily increase my praying about it; I just exercise more faith."

This preacher was expressing the confidence, the boldness, our Scrip-ture text is talking about, because he knew the will of God in the matter.

Some people, on the other hand, only look at the circumstances. They say, "No one came to the altar for salvation last night. They probably won't tonight, either." This kind of person is looking at the wrong thing. He may pray for souls, but he does not see them coming to Christ. He really doesn't have confidence that they will come. His faith is only in what he can see.

We Can Nullify Our Prayers

Often people undo their prayers! They may have prayed and even asked others to pray, but then they nullify their prayers and the faith of those who are praying with them by speaking negatively. Talk *faith*, not *doubt!*

I once knew a minister who asked me and others to pray for his son. However, at the same time he was requesting prayer, he would tell his boy, "You'll never amount to anything. I don't know what in the world I'm going to do with you! I have done everything I can do. I have prayed and prayed, but it looks like my prayers don't do any good."

This man was confessing defeat and failure rather than victory and faith. He was building doubt and insecurity into his son. This is why so many people have lost their children.

As we pray for our children, we must not do anything in our home that would nullify the effects of our prayers. We must build confidence and trust in our children. We must instill a sense of security in them.

Before I was married, I usually stayed in the homes of pastors during revival meetings, and I often felt sorry for their children.

I particularly remember one pastor's 12-year-old son. His parents were impatient and short-tempered with him. They were always telling him he would never amount to anything. Sure enough, he didn't! He broke the hearts of his parents. He was married several times, and he never provided a living for his family.

These parents may have prayed and asked their church to pray. They may have shed many tears and even fasted. But their lives nullified the effects of their prayers.

From the spiritual standpoint as well as the natural standpoint, the things that happen to children in their early years are what mold their lives as adults. Let these years be spiritually rich and meaningful for your children. Let your life match your words. Work with God; don't work against Him.

I also have seen pastors' children neglected. The pastors' wives were so busy working in the church that their children were left alone to do as they pleased. That's why I told my wife when we were first married, "I'll run the church and you run the house."

In the first church we pastored after we were married, we were told it was their custom for the pastor to teach the adult Bible class of men and the pastor's wife to teach the women. I told them my wife didn't teach Sunday School.

They argued, "But it's our custom here. We have been doing this for more than 20 years!"

"Well, I just changed that custom." I replied. "We'll consolidate the two classes and make one big auditorium class, and I will teach it. My wife doesn't teach Sunday School."

When they asked me why, I told them, "I am going to preach and pastor the church. My wife is going to stay home and keep house and take care of me and our children, when we have them. I want her to run things there, and I'll run things here. There are many capable people in the church who can work, so let's put them to work."

When they wanted to make Oretha president of the women's missionary council, I put my foot down again. "She can attend the meetings," I told them, "but she won't serve in any capacity." This has paid off well for us.

Authority To Claim Your Family

Every believer has authority in his own household. We have more authority there than we have anywhere else. Acts 16:31 tells us, *". . . Believe on the Lord Jesus Christ and thou shalt be saved, AND THY HOUSE "* Too many people, in praying for their family, have struggled and begged God to save them, but they have not backed up their prayers by claiming the promise. Thus, they have prayed in darkness instead of in the light of God's Word.

Our text says, *". . . if we ask any thing according to his will* [we know that salvation for our children is God's will], *he heareth us: And if we know that he hear us . . . we know that we have the petitions that we desired of him"* (1 John 5:14,15).

If we *know* God heard us, we don't have to keep begging Him to save our children. This doesn't mean that the whole family will come to Christ overnight, but as we stand in faith, thanking God, they will be saved.

For us to continue asking and begging God is a confession that we don't believe we have our petition. If we really believed we had the petition we desired of the Lord, as the Scripture says, we would be thanking Him for it!

Sometimes, you see, we go through the right motions but without the right believing. We can go through the motions because some-one told us to do so or because someone else did it, but for it to work, we must have faith for the answer down in our hearts.

The thought never entered my mind that our children would not be saved, because I had authority and power in that area. I prayed for them once and claimed their salvation on the basis of the Word. When the thought would come to me that they might not be saved, I would reject it immediately in the Name of Jesus. I had confidence — I had boldness — that our children would be saved because I had prayed according to God's will.

Knowing what the will of God is concerning lost souls, we never should pray, "Lord, if it be your will, save this person." We *know* it is His will!

Memory Text:

"And this is the confidence that we have in him, that, if we ask any thing according to his will, he heareth us: And if we know that he hear us, whatsoever we ask, we know that we have the petitions that we desired of him."

— 1 John 5:14,15

The Will of God In Prayer (Part 2)

Bible Texts: Isaiah 53:4,5; Matthew 8:16,17; 1 Peter 2:24

Central Truth: To be an effective prayer warrior, we must have God's Word abiding in us.

As we continue our study about God's will in prayer, let us look at these pertinent words of Jesus in John 15:7: *"If ye abide in me, and my words abide in you, ye shall ask what ye will and it shall be done unto you."*

Under what conditions did Jesus tell us to ask what we will? He said, *"If ye abide in me. . . ."* In other words, to be born again is the first requirement. If we are born again, we are abiding in Him.

He also said, *". . . and my words abide in you. . . ."* So we must have a thorough knowledge of God's Word to be an effective prayer warrior. We must have His Word abiding in us. In order to do this we must *"Study to shew thyself approved unto God, a workman that needeth not to be ashamed, rightly dividing the word of truth"* (2 Tim. 2:15).

When we have God's Word abiding in us, we will know what His will is concerning any matter we need to pray about. As we saw in our last lesson, *God's Word is His will.* Therefore, we can bring our petitions with confidence and boldness to God's throne of grace.

If we have followed steps one and two of the above verse — if (1) we are abiding in Him, and (2) His Word is abiding in us — we can *"ask what ye will and it shall be done unto you."* What a powerful promise!

The believer walking in fellowship with the Word never will ask for anything outside of the will of God. If he knows the Word, he knows what is promised him; he knows the will of God. If he is not walking in fellowship with the Word, he is not going to have a successful prayer life and get answers to his prayers. His prayer life isn't going to be effective, because Jesus plainly stated, *"If ye abide in me, and my words abide in you. . . ."* We must come according to His conditions.

God's Will Concerning Healing

What does God's Word have to say about physical healing? Is it His will to heal the sick? Let us look at some scriptures to determine His will in this matter.

ISAIAH 63-4,5
4 Surely he hath borne our griefs, and carried our sorrows: yet we did esteem him stricken, smitten of God, and afflicted.
5 But he was wounded for our transgressions, he was bruised for our iniquities: the chastisement of our peace was upon him; and with his stripes we are healed.

MATTHEW 8:16,17
16 When the even was come, they brought unto him many that were possessed with devils: and he cast out the spirits with his word, and healed all that were sick:
17 That it might be fulfilled which was spoken by Esaias the prophet, saying, Himself took our infirmities, and bare our sicknesses.

1 PETER 2:24
24 Who his own self bare our sins in his own body on the tree, that we,
being dead to sins, should live unto righteousness: by whose stripes ye were healed.

We see from these verses that healing the sick is God's will because Christ bore our infirmities and carried our diseases. Just as He purchased our salvation through His death on the cross, so He has purchased our healing: *". . . by whose stripes ye were healed."* When we have His Word firmly settled in our hearts, we need not wonder if it is His will to heal us. We need not pray, "Lord, heal me *if* it be thy will."

Years ago while pastoring, I was called to pray for one of the members who was ill. Knowing the importance of her own confession of faith for healing, I asked, "Sister, will you be healed now as I anoint you with oil and lay hands on you in Jesus' Name?"

"Well, I will if it's God's will," she answered.

"How are you going to find out if it's His will?" I asked.

I thought you would pray for me, and if it's His will, I'll be healed. If it isn't, I won't."

Under these circumstances I knew the woman was not going to receive healing. I knew her unbelief would stop the flow of God's healing power. I wanted to talk to her and show her some things from the Word of God before I prayed for her, but she said, "Go ahead and pray for me. I am in so much pain and misery."

I anointed her and prayed, knowing in my heart that she wouldn't receive anything because she wasn't believing in line with the Word. I stumbled through a prayer and had hardly said, "amen" when she said to her husband, "Pete, go call the doctor."

The thing that really puzzled me was that she had just gotten through saying if it was God's will for her to be healed, He would heal her and if it wasn't, He wouldn't. She didn't get healed; therefore, by her own admission, it *wasn't* God's will for her to be healed. Yet here she was calling the doctor and paying him to get her out of the will of God!

According to her reasoning, it would seem she wouldn't even *want* to get well, because she would be getting out of God's will. It would be wrong to buy medicine and enlist the help of the doctor to get her out of the will of God.

Certainly this is a foolish line of reasoning, but this is the logic some people follow concerning prayer for their healing.

As we noted before, if we want to know God's will concerning a matter, study His Word. His Word is His will. His Word tells us it *is* His will to heal

us. Let's not doubt His Word, but instead claim its promises for our healing.

Look to the Word for God's Will

Many people try to find the will of God by saying, "If it's His will He'll do it, and if it's not, He won't." We should determine God's will by looking into the Word.

If I am uncertain about something, I go to the Word first. I don't pray in uncertainty, because I would be wasting my time. I could not pray in faith; I would be praying in unbelief and doubt, and it wouldn't work. When we know what God's Word says about a matter, we *know* what His will is.

Often people want to put all the responsibility for a matter on God, so they say, "It must not have been God's will, because I prayed, 'If it be thy will, do this,' and He didn't do it." These people want to relieve themselves of all responsibility and put it on God. But we can't get out of it that easily.

God gave us His Word and told us to *"Search the scriptures . . . which testify of me"* (John 5:39). In them we learn His will.

Then there are those who know what God's Word says about a matter, yet they find it difficult to believe it will work in their case.

59

They are like a man who knows he will need some extra money, so he goes to his banker and arranges for a loan. He does not need the money right away; he just wants to have everything ready so he will have access to it when he needs it.

The man has his banker's word that everything is in order and he may pick up the money anytime he wants, but then he thinks *What if he doesn't give it to me? What if he didn't mean what he said?*

The man will have to *believe* what the banker said and then *act on it* to get his money.

Some people are like that with God. They know what He said in His Word about salvation for their loved ones, healing, or any other need they might have, but they find it difficult to believe He will do what He said He would do. But thank God, He keeps His Word!

✳

Memory Text:

"If ye abide in me, and my words abide in you, ye shall ask what ye will and it shall be done unto you."

— John 15:7

The Will of God
In Prayer
(Part 3)

Bible Texts: 1 Peter 5:7; 3 John 2; Philippians 4:19

Central Truth: We can find a promise in God's Word for every aspect of life. Then we can know how to pray, and we can have the assurance before we pray what His will is.

Studying God's Word is like searching for valuable gems. We can find a few jewels on top of the ground without much digging, but if we really want to get down where the valuable veins are, we have to dig for them.

To learn the deeper truths of God, we are told to *"Search the scriptures, for in them ye think ye have eternal life: and they are they which testify of me"* (John 5:39).

Surface reading of our memory text in First John 5:14,15 has brought some to the wrong conclusion about what John was saying here. He said, *"And this is the confidence that we have in him, that, if we ask any thing according to his will he heareth us: And if we know that he hear us, whatsoever we ask, we know* *that we have the petitions that we desired of him."*

Some have thought John said, "If it is God's will, He will hear me, and if it isn't, He won't." However, that wasn't what he meant. John was saying if we have God's Word on a matter, we don't have to say, "If it be thy will," because we know His Word is His will.

For this reason I encourage people to find scriptures with a promise concerning what they are praying about. Sometimes when people ask me to pray for them I say, "What scripture are you standing on?" Many times they answer they have none in particular. "Well," I tell them, "that is what you'll get, then: nothing in particular."

If your request is in accordance with God's Word, that is His will. (It has to be His will for Him to promise it in His Word.) It is His will that we have everything He has provided for us in His Word.

I have found a promise in His Word for every aspect of life. That means I can know just how to pray, and I can have the assurance of what His will is before I pray.

Many times the reason prayer isn't working for people is because they are praying in darkness. They are trying to get God to help them apart from the Word. We are to walk in the light of the Word.

No one can build a successful prayer life if he doesn't know the Word. A successful prayer life is built and based on the written Word. When we pray according to the Word, it is a lamp unto our feet and a light unto our path. We know which way to walk.

Too much of the time, however, because we fail to see what God's Word has to say about a subject, we stumble about, not knowing just where we are going. Prayer then becomes a matter of desperation, begging God to do something. But when we know the Word ahead of time, we can come to God with confidence.

God's Will Concerning Worry

1 PETER 5:7

7 Casting all your care upon him; for he careth for you.

A woman with a look of desperation on her face once came to me requesting prayer. She began crying as she said, "Brother Hagin, the cares of life, the anxieties and worries, are just so great." She began to cry harder as she said, "I just can't carry all my burdens. I want you to pray that God will do one of two things: that He will either give me grace to carry them or else take about half of them away. I can carry half of them, but I just can't carry all of them."

"Well, I can't pray that prayer," I told her. "It would be unscriptural." A bewildered look came across her face. I went on to explain, "I cannot pray for you out of the will of God. If I am going to have any confidence that God will hear my prayer, I must pray in line with the Word of God.

"The Bible tells us, *'And this is the confidence that we have in him, that, if we ask any thing according to his will he heareth us: And if we know that he hear us, whatsoever we ask we know that we have the petitions that we desired of him.'*

"I know God's will for you because I know what God's Word says. It isn't His will to give you grace to bear your load of care. Nor is it His will to take half of it away and let you carry the other half. How do I know this? Because of what His Word says.

"First Peter 5:7 says, *'Casting all your care upon him for he careth for* you.' That verse doesn't say to cast half of your cares; it says all. That verse doesn't say God will give you grace to carry your worries; it says to cast all your care upon Him. Why? Because *'He careth for you.'* "

Then I said, "Sister, isn't it wonderful that we already have the answer for your prayer right here?"

Then I read her this same verse from *The Amplified Bible*, which is more explicit: "Casting the whole of your care — all your anxieties, all your worries, all your concerns, once and for all — on Him; for He cares for you affectionately, and cares about you watchfully."

God's Will Concerning Financial Blessing

3 JOHN 2
2 Beloved, I wish above all things that thou mayest prosper and be in health, even as thy soul prospereth.

PHILIPPIANS 4:19
19 But my God shall supply all your need according to his riches in glory by Christ Jesus.

In Paul's letter to the Church at Philippi, he was commending the Christians for their generosity in giving, as we see in the verses just preceding the above verse. They had taken up an offering of money and goods to send to other Christians. Because of this, Paul was saying to them, "Because you have given to them and helped them, God shall supply all your needs." He was talking about material and financial matters.

Another verse we think of in connection with financial blessing is found in Luke 6:38: *"Give, and it shall be given unto you; good measure, pressed down, and shaken together, and running over, shall men give into your bosom. For with the same measure that ye mete withal it shall be measured to you again."* We often hear this verse quoted when an offering is being taken. The emphasis usually is on "give" in the first part of the verse. But let's not overlook the results of that giving: *". . . it shall be given unto you. . . ."* Thus, we see financial blessings promised in this verse.

Would you like to see increased financial blessings in *your* life? Increase your giving, because the Scripture says that your returns will be *". . . pressed down, and shaken together, and running over. . . . For with the same measure that ye mete withal it shall be measured to you again."*

On the other hand, we can hinder our prayers for financial prosperity by not cooperating with God; by not entering into the doors God opens for us.

I knew a young, able-bodied fellow who was without work for

quite some time. He had a wife and five children. People in the church they attended helped by taking them groceries and clothes for the children. The church women also helped all they could by giving ironing and other work to his wife so she could earn a little money.

When I talked to the man he told me, "Well, the Lord said He would meet all of our needs. Some people tell me to get out and look for a job, but I am just waiting for the right one to come to me. The Lord will do it. And in the meantime, we are getting along all right." (But someone else was paying his house rent and feeding his family.)

We can't just sit and wait for something to come to us. The only thing that will come will be a pile of bills. A man can believe that God will help him and bless him financially, but he needs to move in the right direction and do whatever his hand finds to do.

If the first job he finds isn't exactly what he prefers, at least it will help him until something better comes along. In the meantime he can pray for guidance in getting a better job. God can open another job for him as he is faithful in whatever he finds to do in providing for his family.

As we continue to dig deeper into God's Word, we will see more and more things showing us His will in prayer.

For example, we know to pray for the lost in heathen lands, because His Word says, *"Ask of me, and I shall give thee the heathen for thine inheritance, and the uttermost parts of the earth for thy possession"* (Ps. 2:8).

We also know to pray that God would send ministers forth in the power of His Spirit: *"Pray ye therefore the Lord of the harvest, that he will send forth labourers into his harvest"* (Matt. 9:38).

As we study the Word of God, instead of saying "according to the *will* of God," we will say "according to the *Word* of God." Then we will have the right perspective.

Memory Text:

"And this is the confidence that we have in him, that, if we ask any thing according to his will, he heareth us: And if we know that he hear us, whatsoever we ask, we know that we have the petitions that we desired of him."

— 1 John 5:14,16

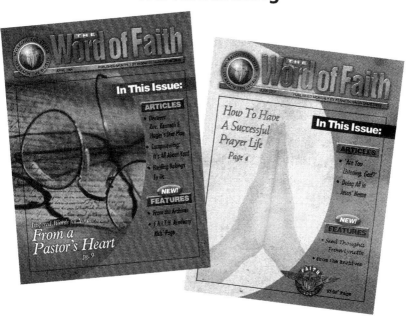

The Word of Faith is a full-color magazine
with faith-building teaching articles by
Rev. Kenneth E. Hagin and Rev. Kenneth Hagin Jr.

The Word of Faith also includes encouraging true-life
stories of Christians overcoming circumstances
through God's Word, and information on the
various outreaches of Kenneth Hagin Ministries
and RHEMA Bible Church.

To receive a free subscription to *The Word of Faith*, call:
1-888-28-FAITH
(1-888-283-2484)
www.rhema.org

RHEMA
Bible Training Center

Want to reach the height of your potential?

RHEMA can take you there.

| proven instructors
| alumni benefits
| career placement
| hands-on experience
| curriculum you can use

Do you desire —

- to find and effectively fulfill God's plan for your life?
- to know how to "rightly divide the Word of truth"?
- to learn how to follow and flow with the Spirit of God?
- to run your God-given race with excellence and integrity?
- to become not only a laborer but a *skilled* laborer?

If so, then RHEMA Bible Training Center is here for you!

For a free video and full-color catalog, call:

1-888-28-FAITH
(1-888-283-2484)

www.rhema.org

RHEMA Bible Training Center admits students of any race, color, or ethnic origin.